You Can Ge

By Liza Charles

ISBN: 978-1-339-02787-6

Art Director: Tannaz Fassihi; Designer: Tanya Chernyak
Photos © Getty Images and Shutterstock.com.

1 2 3 4 5 6 7 8 9 10   68   32 31 30 29 28 27 26 25 24 23

Printed in Jiaxing, China. First printing, August 2023.

Jobs, jobs, jobs!
These people have jobs!
What job will you get
when you are their age?

You can get a job with a badge.
You can help save a life.

3

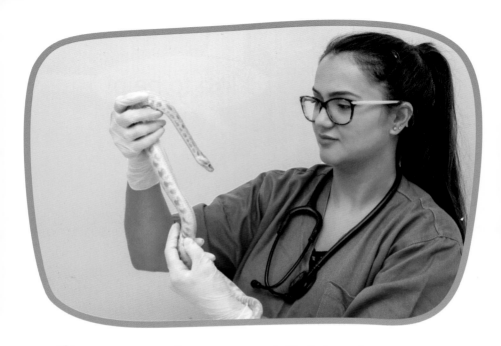

Can you be a vet? Yes!
You can take a snake from
a cage and help it get well.

You can act on a stage.

You can make fudge in a shop. Yum, yum!

You can plan a bridge.
Then, you can make it real
so people can use it.

You can be a judge.

You can get paid a wage
to drive a huge truck.

You can write the pages
of a book like this.
It is such a fun job!